Stanko Radmilovic

Macroeconomic comparative analysis of pre-crisis (2000-07) and the crisis period (2008-12)

For a large sample of countries (70). Part I Numerical factography

GRIN Verlag

Bibliografische Information der Deutschen Nationalbibliothek:

Die Deutsche Bibliothek verzeichnet diese Publikation in der Deutschen National-
bibliografie; detaillierte bibliografische Daten sind im Internet über http://dnb.d-
nb.de/ abrufbar.

Imprint:

Copyright © 2013 GRIN Verlag GmbH
Druck und Bindung: Books on Demand GmbH, Norderstedt Germany
ISBN: 978-3-656-59245-7

GRIN - Your knowledge has value

Der GRIN Verlag publiziert seit 1998 wissenschaftliche Arbeiten von Studenten, Hochschullehrern und anderen Akademikern als eBook und gedrucktes Buch. Die Verlagswebsite www.grin.com ist die ideale Plattform zur Veröffentlichung von Hausarbeiten, Abschlussarbeiten, wissenschaftlichen Aufsätzen, Dissertationen und Fachbüchern.

Visit us on the internet:

http://www.grin.com/

http://www.facebook.com/grincom

http://www.twitter.com/grin_com

Prof. dr Stanko Radmilovic, Novi Sad, Serbia

Macroeconomic comparative analysis of pre-crisis (2000-07) and the crisis period (2008-12) for a large sample of countries (70) - Part I: Numerical factography

Due to the size of this article - numerical factography, Part II - Problemic elaboration of comparative and inter-dependent relationship, the comprehensively treated in a separate articles in the Serbian language   in category Srbija i uže i šire okruženje on the site http://radmilovicstanko.com/.

Country	Subject Descriptor - Averages								
	GDP, constant prices, % change	GDP per capita, current prices, US$	Total investment, % of GDP	Gross national savings, % of GDP	Inflat., aver. consum. prices	Unemploy., %b of tot. lab. forc.	Gen. gov. tot. expend., % of GDP	Gen. gov. gross debt, % of GDP	Curr. acc. bal. - defic/sufic., % of GDP
1	2	3	4	5	6	7	8	9	10
Albania 2000-07	6,0	2.125,0	28,5	22,9	2,7	14,9	30,1	60,9	-5,6
Albania 2008-12	3,7	3.907,0	28,0	15,5	2,9	13,6	30,2	58,2	-12,5
Angola 2000-07	12,4	1.421,0	12,4	19,8	97,1	0,0	40,4	62,7	6,6
Angola 2008-12	5,5	9.535,0	24,1	23,1	9,0	7,7	39,2	51,2	0,9
Argentina 2000-07	3,5	5.313,0	18,1	20,8	8,9	15,0	31,8	95,2	2,6
Argentina 2008-12	5,5	9.535,0	24,1	23,1	9,0	7,7	39,2	51,2	0,9
Australia 2000-07	3,4	29.782,0	26,3	21,7	3,2	5,6	34,5	13,4	-4,8
Australia 2008-12	2,5	56.845,0	27,9	24,4	2,8	5,1	36,3	20,1	-3,5
Austria 2000-07	2,4	32.807,0	23,1	24,8	1,9	4,4	50,8	64,5	1,7
Austria 2008-12	0,6	47.597,0	22,3	25,0	2,3	4,3	51,2	70,2	2,7
Azerbaijan 2000-07	15,9	1.486,0	35,0	30,8	6,2	5,9	24,6	18,0	-3,5
Azerbaijan 2008-12	5,5	6.141,0	20,2	46,8	7,4	6,1	33,7	10,4	26,7
Belarus 2000-07	7,8	2.433,0	28,1	24,9	43,1	2,0	42,9	11,9	-3,2
Belarus 2008-12	5,0	6.092,0	39,8	30,1	29,6	0,7	43,7	35,8	-9,7
Belgium 2000-07	2,2	31.602,0	21,3	24,3	2,1	7,7	49,6	96,7	3,0
Belgium 2008-12	0,4	45.197,0	21,5	20,9	2,6	7,5	52,8	95,6	-0,5
B - H 2000-07	4,7	2.433,0	26,2	12,9	2,7	30,8	48,6	27,4	-13,4
B - H 2008-12	0,8	4.525,0	19,5	10,8	3,0	26,1	49,7	38,2	-9,1
Brazil 2000-07	3,5	4.254,0	17,1	16,6	7,3	10,4	37,6	70,4	-0,5
Brazil 2008-12	3,2	10.552,0	19,2	17,3	5,5	6,8	39,0	65,8	-2,0
Bulgaria 2000-07	5,7	3.114,0	24,4	14,5	6,6	13,2	35,9	44,5	-9,9
Bulgaria 2008-12	0,7	6.801,0	27,1	20,3	4,6	9,3	35,5	16,0	-6,8
Canada 2000-07	2,8	31.576,0	21,6	23,3	2,3	7,0	39,8	75,4	1,7
Canada 2008-12	1,2	47.679,0	23,4	20,8	1,8	7,4	41,6	80,9	-2,6

Chile 2000-07	4,7	6.557,0	21,7	22,7	3,1	9,1	21,4	10,2	1,0
Chile 2008-12	3,9	12.710,0	23,4	22,5	3,6	8,1	23,4	8,3	-0,9
China 2000-07	10,5	1.538,0	40,1	44,6	1,7	3,9	18,4	18,0	4,5
China 2008-12	9,3	4.615,0	47,0	51,7	3,3	4,2	23,0	23,3	4,7
Croatia 2000-07	4,6	8.463,0	26,5	21,3	2,9	13,5	42,6	35,7	-5,2
Croatia 2008-12	-1,8	14.011,0	24,2	20,9	3,0	11,6	42,3	42,3	-3,3
Cyprus 2000-07	3,8	19.519,0	18,9	13,3	2,7	4,5	41,6	65,7	-5,5
Cyprus 2008-12	0,2	28.651,0	18,7	9,5	2,7	7,2	45,3	65,2	-9,2
Czech R. 2000-07	4,7	10.615,0	28,2	24,0	2,6	7,6	43,8	26,4	-4,2
Czech R. 2008-12	0,3	19.737,0	25,3	22,5	2,8	6,4	43,5	36,9	-2,8
Denmark 2000-07	1,9	41.575,0	21,1	23,9	2,1	4,6	53,7	42,6	2,8
Denmark 2008-12	-0,9	58.387,0	18,2	22,8	2,4	6,4	56,6	42,7	4,6
Estonia 2000-07	8,2	8.694,0	33,2	22,6	4,1	9,3	34,4	4,9	-10,6
Estonia 2008-12	-0,7	15.836,0	24,2	23,8	4,5	11,6	44,3	6,6	-0,4
Finland 2000-07	3,5	33.074,0	20,7	26,6	1,6	8,6	49,1	41,6	5,9
Finland 2008-12	-0,5	47.040,0	19,8	20,4	2,7	7,7	54,2	45,7	0,5
France 2000-07	2,1	30.905,0	19,8	20,3	1,8	8,9	52,8	62,1	0,5
France 2008-12	0,0	42.794,0	20,1	18,4	1,7	9,4	55,8	81,2	-1,8
Germany 2000-07	1,7	30.269,0	18,9	22,1	1,7	9,4	46,5	64,1	3,2
Germany 2008-12	0,7	42.173,0	17,7	24,1	1,8	6,8	46,1	77,3	6,3
Greece 2000-07	4,1	18.563,0	23,6	15,1	3,3	10,0	45,6	102,6	-8,4
Greece 2008-12	-4,4	26.458,0	18,0	8,2	2,9	14,3	51,6	143,8	-9,8
Hungary 2000-07	3,6	8.769,0	24,7	18,2	6,4	6,5	50,0	59,6	-7,5
Hungary 2008-12	-0,9	13.482,0	19,7	18,9	4,9	10,3	49,8	79,0	-0,8
India 2000-07	7,1	642,9	29,4	29,3	4,6	0,0	26,8	79,6	-0,1
India 2008-12	6,8	1.309,1	35,8	32,5	9,9	0,0	28,0	70,0	-3,2
Indonesia 2000-07	5,0	1.196,0	23,9	26,8	8,8	9,2	19,5	60,0	2,9
Indonesia 2008-12	5,9	2.920,0	31,9	31,9	5,9	7,2	19,1	27,4	0,0
Iran 2000-07	6,0	2.530,0	34,1	40,2	13,9	12,7	21,6	22,1	6,1
Iran 2008-12	2,3	5.846,0	36,2	42,7	20,1	12,1	21,6	13,8	6,5
Ireland 2000-07	5,8	41.485,0	24,8	22,9	3,5	4,4	33,2	29,9	-1,9
Ireland 2008-12	-1,2	49.615,0	13,7	13,6	0,6	12,3	48,9	85,0	-0,2
Israel 2000-07	3,9	20.373,0	18,6	19,6	1,5	11,6	50,8	90,5	1,1
Israel 2008-12	3,6	29.752,0	17,0	19,0	3,2	7,8	44,7	76,3	2,0
Italy 2000-07	1,6	26.975,0	21,2	20,6	2,4	8,1	47,5	105,7	-0,6
Italy 2008-12	-1,4	35.520,0	19,5	17,1	2,4	8,4	50,3	117,9	-2,4
Japan 2000-07	1,5	34.414,0	23,1	26,4	-0,3	4,7	35,3	170,4	3,3
Japan 2008-12	-0,1	42.589,0	20,6	23,2	-0,2	4,6	39,3	217,2	2,6
Kazakh. 2000-07	10,2	3.144,0	29,6	27,2	8,5	9,1	21,6	10,8	-2,4
Kazakh. 2008-12	4,8	9.639,0	25,9	28,8	9,0	6,0	23,6	10,1	2,9
Korea 2000-07	5,2	15.174,0	29,7	32,0	3,0	3,7	20,1	24,0	2,3

Korea 2008-12	2,9	20.413,0	28,8	31,5	3,3	3,5	21,8	33,0	2,6
Latvia 2000-07	6,3	6.322,6	31,1	18,8	5,0	10,3	35,8	12,3	-12,2
Latvia 2008-12	7,3	13.241,9	24,6	23,5	4,8	14,9	41,2	32,7	-1,1
Lithuan. 2000-07	7,5	6.389,0	22,8	15,0	1,9	11,2	34,0	20,2	-7,8
Lithuan. 2008-12	-0,2	12.913,0	18,8	16,0	4,8	13,2	39,7	32,2	-2,8
Maced. 2000-07	3,0	2.573,0	0,0	16,6	2,6	34,5	35,6	38,6	-5,1
Maced. 2008-12	1,9	4.751,0	0,0	21,1	3,3	32,1	32,5	26,1	-5,7
Mexico 2000-07	2,8	7.779,0	24,5	23,1	5,2	3,3	22,2	41,5	-1,5
Mexico 2008-12	1,7	9.533,0	24,9	24,1	4,4	5,0	26,8	43,6	-0,8
Moldova 2000-07	5,7	687,0	27,5	20,9	13,4	7,4	35,1	54,4	-6,6
Moldova 2008-12	3,0	1.772,0	26,7	16,2	6,5	6,0	41,4	23,8	-10,5
Montene. 2000-07	4,8	3.397,0	21,6	6,1	19,7	0,0	40,4	43,3	-20,3
Montene. 2008-12	1,4	6.818,0	26,1	-3,8	4,0	0,0	46,1	41,0	-27,2
Netherl. 2000-07	2,2	34.465,0	20,1	25,6	2,5	3,9	45,6	50,5	5,5
Netherl. 2008-12	0,0	48.967,0	18,4	25,5	1,9	4,2	49,5	63,9	7,0
N. Zealand 2000-07	3,7	21.502,0	22,9	17,6	2,6	4,6	33,9	24,6	-5,5
N. Zealand 2008-12	0,7	33.190,0	19,8	15,1	2,7	6,1	38,0	30,7	-4,7
Nigeria 2000-07	9,3	678,0	24,6	31,4	12,4	13,1	31,6	51,3	6,9
Nigeria 2008-12	6,9	1.426,0	25,1	32,8	12,2	19,9	27,2	15,5	7,7
Norway 2000-07	2,4	55.612,0	20,9	35,0	1,9	3,8	43,2	45,8	14,2
Norway 2008-12	0,6	91.388,0	23,8	37,1	2,1	3,2	43,5	44,3	13,3
Pakistan 2000-07	5,3	654,0	18,5	18,6	5,4	7,3	18,2	70,7	0,1
Pakistan 2008-12	3,0	1.105,0	16,3	12,6	12,6	6,0	20,6	61,1	-3,6
Peru 2000-07	5,1	2.674,0	19,3	19,0	2,2	9,0	19,0	40,0	-0,3
Peru 2008-12	6,5	5.295,0	25,2	22,6	3,5	7,8	19,7	24,0	-2,5
Philippin. 2000-07	4,9	1.182,0	20,8	21,8	4,6	10,4	20,4	58,8	1,0
Philippin. 2008-12	4,7	2.185,0	19,5	23,1	4,8	7,3	18,9	43,2	3,6
Poland 2000-07	4,1	6.870,0	21,0	17,0	3,4	16,8	43,2	43,6	-4,0
Poland 2008-12	3,4	12.675,0	21,6	16,8	3,6	9,0	44,0	52,9	-4,8
Portugal 2000-07	1,5	16.088,0	24,8	15,4	3,0	6,2	44,2	57,6	-9,3
Portugal 2008-12	-1,1	22.034,0	19,5	10,8	1,9	11,3	48,1	95,8	-8,5
Qatar 2000-07	12,0	41.533,0	31,5	56,5	5,9	0,0	29,1	32,2	25,1
Qatar 2008-12	13,2	82.384,0	29,4	54,5	2,3	0,0	30,2	31,1	25,1
Romania 2000-07	5,7	3.749,0	23,7	17,0	18,8	7,3	33,2	21,6	-7,2
Romania 2008-12	0,4	8.261,0	27,2	21,5	5,7	6,9	37,3	28,0	-5,7
Russia 2000-07	7,2	4.330,0	20,8	31,1	14,2	8,2	33,3	29,0	10,3
Russia 2008-12	1,9	11.691,0	22,4	27,2	9,2	7,0	37,2	10,5	4,8
Sau. Arab. 2000-07	4,7	11.940,0	21,5	37,4	0,8	10,3	33,9	61,4	15,9
Sau. Arab. 2008-12	6,6	20.810,0	28,7	46,9	4,1	10,7	35,2	8,7	18,2
Serbia 2000-07	5,1	2.879,0	18,8	11,1	25,9	17,1	42,1	89,2	-7,7
Serbia 2008-12	0,2	5.508,0	20,9	9,8	9,0	19,9	46,4	46,3	-11,0

Slovak R. 2000-07	5,6	7.447,0	27,5	20,9	6,0	16,8	30,9	40,0	-6,9
Slovak R. 2008-12	2,1	16.886,0	22,9	20,4	2,7	12,8	38,1	40,0	-2,5
Slovenia 2000-07	4,4	15.574,0	27,2	25,4	5,3	6,2	42,0	27,3	-1,8
Slovenia 2008-12	-1,0	24.291,0	22,4	21,4	2,6	7,0	45,4	39,0	-1,0
S. Africa 2000-07	4,3	4.141,0	17,5	15,2	5,3	25,4	26,7	36,5	-2,3
S. Africa 2008-12	2,2	6.816,0	20,1	15,5	6,7	24,4	32,1	35,4	-4,7
Spain 2000-07	3,6	22.253,0	28,3	22,5	3,2	10,5	38,8	47,7	-5,8
Spain 2008-12	-0,8	31.694,0	23,4	18,7	2,3	19,2	45,2	61,7	-4,7
Sweden 2000-07	3,2	36.524,0	18,1	24,6	1,5	6,0	51,9	49,8	6,5
Sweden 2008-12	1,1	51.431,0	18,7	26,1	1,6	7,7	50,5	39,4	7,3
Switz. 2000-07	2,2	46.813,0	22,1	0,0	1,0	2,7	35,5	63,7	11,3
Switz. 2008-12	1,2	73.314,0	20,5	0,0	0,4	3,1	32,6	49,4	9,7
Thailand 2000-07	5,1	2.595,0	26,1	29,1	2,5	1,3	21,1	49,8	3,0
Thailand 2008-12	2,9	4.903,0	26,6	29,5	2,9	0,8	23,2	42,2	2,9
Tunisia 2000-07	4,8	2.907,0	24,0	21,2	2,9	14,1	29,3	58,5	-2,7
Tunisia 2008-12	2,5	4.256,0	25,7	20,3	4,4	14,1	32,5	43,0	-5,4
Turkey 2000-07	5,2	5.613,0	19,2	16,1	26,9	9,6	36,3	58,7	-3,1
Turkey 2008-12	3,2	9.980,0	20,1	14,2	8,1	11,2	35,7	40,8	-5,9
Ukraine 2000-07	7,5	1.490,0	22,6	26,3	11,3	8,7	40,5	26,8	3,8
Ukraine 2008-12	-0,6	3.378,0	20,5	15,5	11,8	7,8	48,0	34,1	-5,0
UAEmir. 2000-07	8,0	41.046,0	20,8	30,3	5,2	0,0	18,9	5,1	9,4
UAEmir. 2008-12	2,2	60.028,0	22,2	28,7	3,2	0,0	23,1	18,7	6,5
UK 2000-07	3,2	33.747,0	17,4	15,1	1,6	5,2	38,8	40,5	-2,3
UK 2008-12	-0,4	38.550,0	15,0	13,1	3,3	7,4	45,1	75,1	-1,9
US 2000-07	2,6	40.105,0	19,7	15,5	2,8	5,0	35,6	61,9	-4,9
US 2008-12	0,6	47.485,0	16,0	12,4	2,1	8,3	41,5	94,4	-3,3
Uzbeki. 2000-07	6,0	530,0	24,4	29,2	16,8	0,3	33,2	37,3	4,9
Uzbeki. 2008-12	8,4	1.379,0	30,9	36,0	12,2	0,2	32,4	10,3	5,1
Venez. 2000-07	4,7	5.246,0	23,8	34,6	19,0	13,4	33,0	39,8	10,8
Venez. 2008-12	2,1	12.133,0	24,7	29,5	26,6	8,0	37,1	34,1	4,7
Vietnam 2000-07	7,6	562,0	35,1	33,1	4,7	5,6	26,8	39,3	-2,0
Vietnam 2008-12	5,9	1.238,0	33,8	30,8	13,4	4,5	31,6	50,2	-3,0

Source of data:: IMF WEO Database, April, 2013